3618

Storm Damage

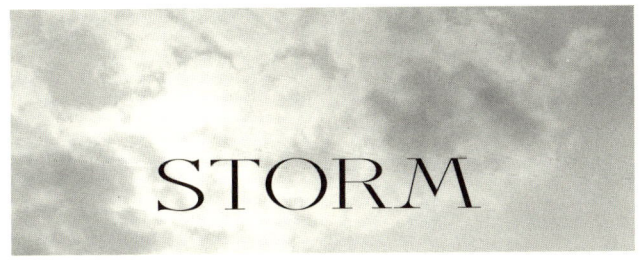

STORM

DAMAGE

꘎꘎꘎

Melissa Hotchkiss

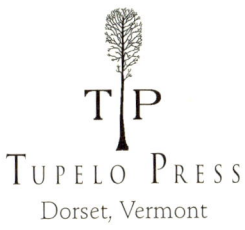

Tupelo Press
Dorset, Vermont

Storm Damage

Copyright © 2002 Melissa Hotchkiss

ISBN 0-9710310-7-X

Printed in Canada

Library of Congress Control Number:
2002102256

First paperback edition 2002

Tupelo Press
PO Box 539, Dorset, Vermont 05251
802.366.8185 • Fax 802.362.1883
editor@tupelopress.org • web www.tupelopress.org

Cover Photograph: H. D. Archibald, ca. 1930's,
near Hamilton's Island, New York
Cover and book design by William Kuch, WK Graphic Design

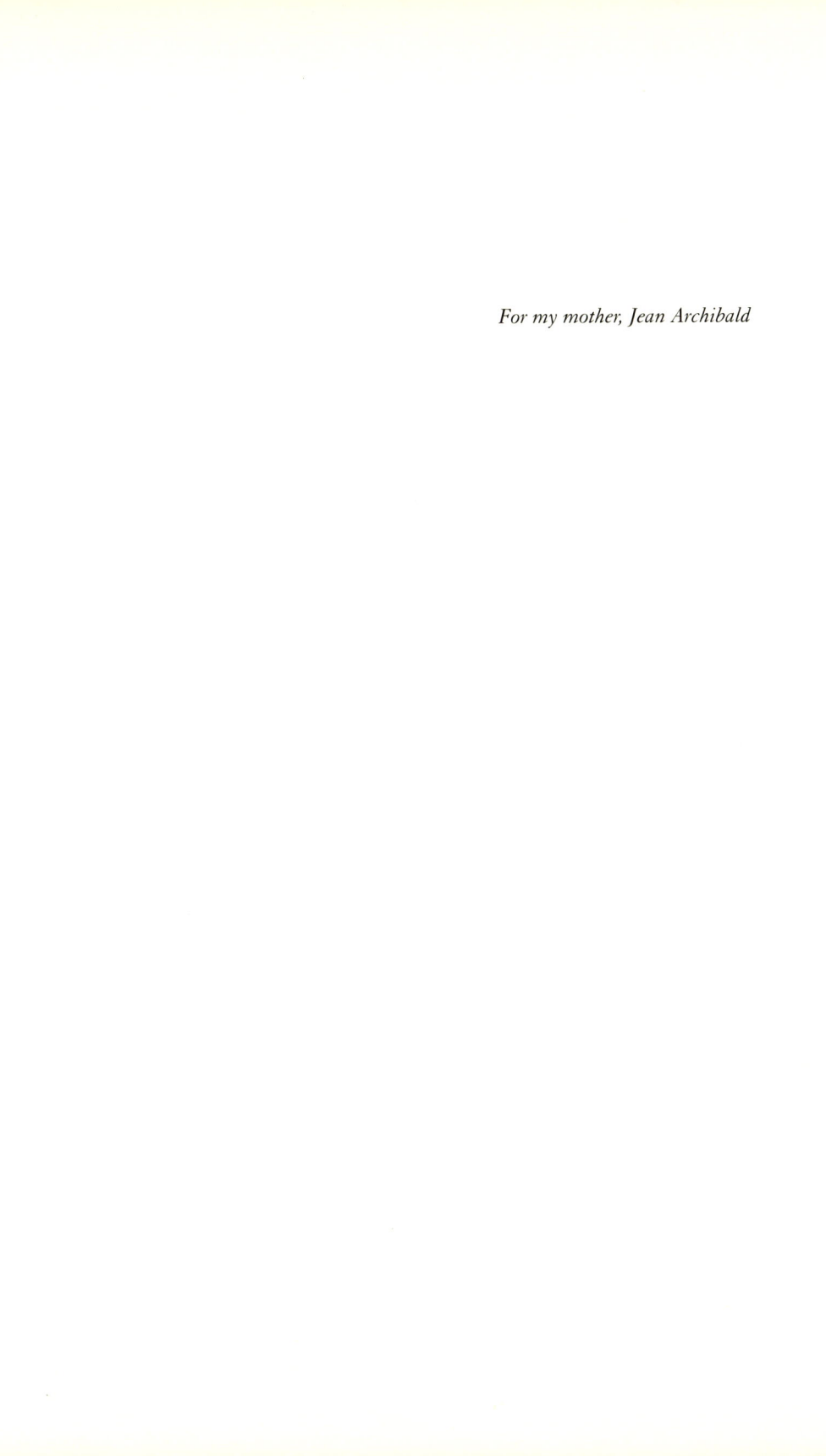

For my mother, Jean Archibald

"Seeing is the effort to create presence:
to possess a thing would be to make it vanish."

- Paul Auster

"...[G]rumbling about an overdue debt will cause the subclan's rainstones to become
aggressive and strike the property of the debtor's subclan with storm damage...
[T]hose who suffered it consult a diviner...After making the necessary oracular enquiries...
the diviner suggests or hints at the particular debt which lies behind the damage..."

- Sir Edward Evans-Pritchard, *Essays in Sudan Ethnography*

❧ CONTENTS ❧

III

IV

I

WHALE BONE

A back bone, impressive and vile
Lying without a body on a beach I happen upon
Not one with sand or happy children but thick marsh and all sorts of rocks

Each vertebra partially sun bleached, though it's foggy now
Each not the same size, smaller and smaller toward the tailbone
(Like our own) all the flesh not really gone

And there's the seaweed draped as in ceremony
Pretty and ugly at the same time, the thresh and wave
Of water giving up what I claim as mine

SACHET

Let's just talk today
The sachet, trapped in the fold of my umbrella
Unnoticed until the street

Then, not even me
A homeless man, wearing clear garbage bags
"Oh, you dropped something"
I say: "It's just a napkin"

Not even realizing the resemblance
(But why would I)
A napkin, more familiar

Now, searching for the dictionary
Largest red book in the house

I'm caught finally in the S's
And see: "semaphore," "sassy bark"
Standing out like signs or danger

MAINE

White with soap
Each arm looking bleached, parched
In the sun
You chose
Only to lather the tops
(Not the pale undersides)
Also, just the fronts of your legs
I stood in the cabin
Wondering
You looked so peculiar
Half done

With bits of light falling onto gray rock
Your shadow stretching
You dove down
Straight
Deep into black water
Soft flurry of bubbles
Leaving an oval, visual caviar
On the floating surface

Your body submerged without light
Quickly, I reached
The door opened into air smelling cool, pine

Folding over in water
Your movements unforced, unrehearsed
The easy sound of your breathing
Creating creases in my skin

THE CHORE

She sent her
To gather mint
For tea

From the kitchen
Watching her daughter
Floating, cartwheels

Toward water
Where leaves soft green
Grow wild

Small hands
Then, into the cool dark brook
Pulling stalks

The mother
Needing a moment
Lets rising steam
Layer the window

A BLUE SKIRT WITH WHITE THIN FLOWERS

Her husband chose
A blue skirt with white thin flowers
Patterned, his love for her obvious
Her repetition of the purchase "Picked this out for me"
Said twice, wrapped around her waist

Nothing like the terry cloth
Turquoise pants my mother wore for years in a row
Shrunk so many times in length
Barely fell half way down the calf

Worn terry cloth not soft
After all the wash
Embarrassed worried
Who cared for her that much

ALL THE KING'S HORSES ALL THE KING'S MEN

Put that back together again
Milk spilled years ago
Or the too many apples eaten
Before each first day of school

Scramble the eggs farther
Sunny Sunday morning
Supposed to make breakfast for your father
Pancake batter sitting longer and longer

Waiting for him to appear as magic
(Understand, a leaf turns every color but what it was)
Instead, wish him dead, dead of something
Everything dies of something

Remember the cracked pot
Glued together in secret?
Or the old storm window
Shattered on the lawn by the water well

It must have been tired, sick and tired of the climb every fall
To a window, cold screaming winters they were
Protecting that thing
Someone called home

And then -
Dragged back down again

STARTING IN

It feels like rain this evening
  just like it did last evening

The weight of the day
  forcing it almost

My street louder than usual

Cars honking longer than usual

Rain starting in on my window
  and the laughing

Kids laughing on the corner—unusual

  Who are those children
  and why aren't they mine

IN THE PARK

a boy in a white T-shirt on a muggy, heavy not quite rainy evening
throws an ice cube, the kind that's round hollow
over a black iron fence

a blue police car, unrelated to this boy, backs up
(a bicycle in its rear trunk)
moves forward as brake lights release

an ice cube a surprise
I rest on worn wooden benches, nothing melts as easily
as a clear ice cube on a muggy evening in June

are the trees leaning? they look strange, full, tall
strong this night while other things which can disappear too do
a small girl creeps one bench further away each minute from her father

holding bright yellow chips in one hand it is there she must belong
waving as he says careful, the bag of chips in the other hand he says
the thing we need repeated most, careful, careful

UNEVEN PAVEMENT

A boomerang into traffic, cover of a tennis ball can
Small arch through rain, mist then steam
Above uneven pavement, so much drizzle and so much cool

What might make a man send a small object into the path
Of a fire truck or city bus?
Happy as it is flying, something comes back done

MORNING

Across the street
Things happen suddenly

A white bag, a tall woman's head
Floating across the avenue, in a strong wind

Her fingers peel the plastic molded to her forehead
Her eyes, her neck, her mouth

From my window I see the bag pitch, turn, like a kite might
Fly, early in its journey from a field, far from the city

She gulps, breathes for air
Not a fish stranded at the bottom of a rowboat in summer
But a gesture, so slight and silent from this perch

Where I only hear my cat eating the dying houseplants again
The dripping of a hand-washed garment in the bathroom

SURGERY

Waiting for the evening breeze
   to move in slowly
   through the screens
   onto the porch, into my chair

Lift me towards the ceiling
   above the light green carpet with its almost invisible yellow lines
   I'll float for hours

From room to room
   following my sisters, their steps quiet when they brush
   their long hair, pulling knots with small dark combs

These scars across my stomach—
   one summer night
The smell of horse manure, cut grass
Running into the fence, in the humid dark
   there were so many bright lights, the doctor's black string
   threading itself, sudden sharpness

I understand why air won't search for a body
   or fill the lungs during a hot spell so long even the artichoke plants are dying
   my hand stops the sun
My hands rip my skin, as I choose to float
   and separate

PLATINUM

Remembering our day in the harbor
My white blisters
Smell of baby seals, maggots crawling from their mouths
Barnacles on stone, sticky seaweed

Stench of rotting skin, against the day
Against the waves
Against the strong salt breeze
Pushing through your gray hairs

Framing those two half-eaten faces
Turning your camera
Calling to me

Shade the light
You said, there's too much light
Too much light

Slowly, with skin turned red orange
My shadow covered their grave

CHINA LAKE

My grandfather, standing in water
    carrying the lake to his face,
    back and forth, over and over
    rubbing his hands

On the shore, parts of my body
    touching hot metal of the green canvas chair

I keep watching him, unable to block
    the sounding waves, or clawing sun

One more thing happens:
    he points towards his feet, signaling

Round golden sunfish nibble his toes
    I know this, he lets them touch him
They tickle, he says, which I never believe
    because I cannot see how this biting doesn't tear—

How he can stand there, letting it happen, wanting it to happen,
Why blood doesn't flow from his feet as he leaves the lake

CLOTH FLOWERS

Cloth flowers on a dress undone by just revealing
What *can* heal or surprise? Not a stark constant sun

She does not collect the dime on the sidewalk
Lost by some other person, she is traveling toward a photo booth

Wants a picture, of herself in love
Although it seems inappropriate to undress

It's not about being naked, and finally her face
Looks discolored, her eyes quite far apart

There is no real difference, only memory
What that alone destroys

II

NEIGHBOR

Bitch, he says, bitch
I am pounding on the floor again
His music in my home

Moving down the stairs, now I am
Begging, almost at his door

It's torture, really, I hear myself saying
You have to understand

Does it really bother you that much?
I say yes
He says fine

Again, as his door closes
Bitch, he says, fucking bitch

TEMPER

Ripping down from their pillows
That morning he decided
To be dramatic

White small feathers
Floating
Softly, with no breeze

Deliberately, the kind of kiss
He gave to her, earlier

Biting, needing
So much to damage

ISOLATION

A blue house with three stories,
the girl in her yellow nightgown
walking out.
Or drowning sea rocks
when high tide just comes along,
takes everything away.

THE BREAKUP

It was walking into the sprinkler
I remember most clearly

Not because of thick water slapping my face
Or the way my dress stuck to my body

But because I was blaming you
My voice was louder than your voice
And I was blaming you

EVENINGS

They did this often
Touching each other
Making love
As if it were final

His cigarettes
On her bare open back
Small round circles of flesh

Calming, methodical
Noises

NOON, APPLES

A dull knife into your mouth
Feeding you, slightly
Lifting your chin
Thinking,
Mother

SUMMER

it seems more than hours and hours
the tide takes to go completely away
far as the moon allows

some things turn kinder as they leave
softer with an exit
routine day of July, the clapboards of the barn baking dry
fading in the sun

time to look for my mother's glasses
lost in the garage near the brown fishing poles
yesterday, wasn't she wearing them there?

*

why won't the sun hide a little
behind the cloud
my mouth wide
when I see the bar of soap my brother brings from the woods
teethed and punctured, a wild animal disappointed by the taste finally found

*

this is the summer of flounder, fourteen in all
heavy dull fish to catch
their eyes most bothered me round blank swollen
compared to the flat rest of them

I am sorry to have selfishly dragged the things from the bottom of the harbor to die
none even put up a fight, piled for my collection in the bow of my red rowboat
resigning that quickly

*

what must have been fog creeping in
never even balked at surrounding our yellow house until dawn
it will stay, the keys from the old truck strong enough to pry
even the top off a dark bottle of root beer

the moving of a fan near the window is not what bothers me
but the distant ache of a lobster boat hauling traps at the end of the day
it will find home too

I know the sounds which are important:
the buzzing of cluster flies between the screen and storm window
a door slamming shut then opening again
mean rain, dying fire

small collapses only small ones
I will understand these only not the absence of a whole
a whole father

*

where has she left them now?
by the fish hooks earlier
lost again, it will only take a while to find

it is empty sea urchins and dead sand dollars I treasure most
bake them on the porch each afternoon the drying sun
I traveled not far to the pond

a sailboat, folded paper, moving origami
from the sandy tiny beach I listen a whole day to nothing
and still feel full

almost time to cook lobsters hear them flip and struggle and quiet
in a pot too small for most anything at all

some say hit them over the head with a hammer it is kinder that way
but the end of the night is always the same -

drag their outer bones to the shore

let the high tide take them away

"...summer. Summer? My memory flutters—"
Emily Dickinson, 1858

Time and memory, one thing
Part past, the other approaching
A word lies before
Decides what sound is after

The hush hush
After the rush
An undertaker's watch still ticking

Arrived not by word of mouth
Instead, a letter

Mother's gone

Does this sound wrong?
Or look much better

What was worst
Mattered most -
The constant hack & cough
Of the old horse

Rattling away in the stall
Was it moldy hay
Eaten last winter?

Or miles covered
At fall's first frost

What belongs together
Nothing apart

Newspapers crawl stone steps
Of a house—this fall, cutting wind—

Like an accordion
They travel farther, down the street

Each sheet moving faster
(Printed weather into choir)

The pitch gets higher
Trees stretch out in branch

As if embrace an answer, instead of happenstance

"Today, makes Yesterday mean."
Emily Dickinson, 1862

Was today, this morning?

Cruel parting of Noon
Hands shake, then separate

Each duel a day—
Rehearsed too soon

III

LIGHTNING

One look—
A strike, fright
This house

White porch
Maple tree—split in two

As if or as like, a lover leaving a place,
He's been allowed
To wander

CHRISTMAS

Lights again, across the street
Red, yellow, green, flashing
On the balcony

A man again, on the corner
Selling trees where last year
He sliced his hand sawing on a day it snowed
People noticed but did not stare

KAYAKING

Waves were only what I wanted
A tiny rock island, half a mile out from shore
Or the small cove before your house
Adding one more quarter mile away

LAST SATURDAY

I am in the driver's seat
My license has expired

My mother keeps repeating
"There is nowhere to plant the zinnias"
Nowhere to plant the zinnias?

Driving to a wedding on a bright clear day
She panics in a crowd of twenty
When she cannot find me

ELIZABETH

My niece has this way
Of holding her face tightly between her hands
Rubbing her fingers across her eyes

I noticed it after her father started stabbing
The dead chicken frying in a pan

Oil forming circles on the stove
My sister was crying

MEDITATION

When he says 'girlfriend'
He could mean

A few dates—

Oor
Six months
In bed!

What does he mean
When he says 'girlfriend'?

UNTITLED

I dream the final wave

Spotting it from shore

Each roll of water

This one, no, that one

By my side, someone saying

"Why do you pretend it is visible?"

IN THE BAHAMAS

A man calls me darling

I see parachutes falling

Sand is colder

I dig my hands farther

He is again

Calling me honey

Under a tree in the sun

IS IT THE OAK LEAF

Is it the oak leaf I'm wanting
With its shape, unlike the kind lines
Of a maple tree leaf?

Or, strong stalks of mint
Growing rapid cool, a brook by a house?

Or maybe the solid paw prints
Of a black barn cat embedded
In the cement garage floor?

Or rather where they lead to:
My father's workshop
The sometimes running table saw
Tore and scratched each slab of wood its highest pitch.

This sound, then no sound
Miss and need after all the nervous cutting wood is gone.

SUNDAY DRIVE

Sunday drive with my father
Scary dirt road, the backside of a small mountain
Northeast of our house
If a place can feel like dusk this place is it

Farther on there's a silo
Must we mention the design
Round, for the grain not to rot it mustn't
The metal belts strained yes but solid

Now the cows are moving in
White and black spots
Slowly we'll get caught
A train crossing
But much more individual
Each has a name

Flies following, their own
Little swarms
Not to be confused with herds

Bushel, gallons, flakes, bales
Pounds, buckets, rakes and nails

A so long ago remember
(I believe you failed)

GNAW AND ECHO OF THE AIRCRAFT

Gnaw and echo of the aircraft long in my ear
After your departure
The airport, sick ward

Wheelchairs empty in the corner
The doors whoosh to each side under the red exit sign

I am entering winter and know the tired ride home
The curves in the road, the pothole past the fat tin mailbox
Eight miles away

You are already gone

And I am what they call strong
I am what
They call competent

But nothing seems enough to stop the clinging to this body
You do so well in it definitive morning even not wanting kisses

What is it—the dream about the pearls
Recurring, bearing round gifts
Wrapped in strands
I do not remember how it unraveled

White, pure, falling
Uncontrollably falling
As if it were me
A child who might yank a necklace
From its mother's breast

Taking what is already taken
As if it were me who could turn such a poison into stone

TRACKS

The tracks make the sound of rocking as the train comes closer
I think of my lover inside me
That same sort of cold, mechanical movement

My body is silent and there are so many sounds I could hear
So much space, if everything were the white I dream
The world would feel quiet

Every room full of clouds, people gulping the color into their lungs
Feeling softer, white white air melting into their bodies

Imagine what it felt like to be surrounded by fluids, to be so close
Only breathe because someone else is breathing

PUNISHMENT

You were dying
   you looked so pale
   your eyes dark lines

Holding so tightly onto your shoes
   rubber soles stretching, over the harbor
   grainy wet salt sand stinging

Sliced finger tips of skin
   your feet growing longer

Every door locked, all chairs empty
   windows fell wide, air touched each stair
   dust was open, every exit at each step

You raised your arms and slapped my face twice as hard

WEEKEND

Do you remember any moment well?

Shiny tan car rented
       cows crossing, staring at the headlights blindly

As if we didn't belong, even in the day their necks
swaying, not attached

Near the end of summer
       the dirt road friendly enough,
          guiding us along—you waved at the farmers

But we had to stop at some point
       (you told me not to watch)

Your back to me,
       urinating into a growing field

I played with the radio,
       pretending to listen

Then there was the lake
       with dying crawfish and cool water, I waded into

IV

RETURN

Who has mentioned clear water right behind the white farmhouse
Who has mentioned a dark gray Dutch door
Who has mentioned tall birch trees growing, will they ever stop growing
Who has mentioned a baby grand piano, chipped ivory keys

These are the things that don't matter
Not food served or the ringing of a phone over blue linoleum
Or a draining, straining sink

Who has mentioned the sucking noise a parent makes with the end of their reading
        glasses after supper
Or the tall knife-like ice fallen from a roof in winter
Who has mentioned no sound at night—does anyone remember
No whispering, no water dripping from a faucet, no doors banging from the wind it
        was quiet

Who has mentioned the maple tree struck by lightning during a summer thunderstorm
Or firewood, rotting near the driveway in April
Who has mentioned a cold perfectly cut granite floor

Who has mentioned a mother driving to the store
For all the ice in the world still unable to stop the nosebleed of a dying white horse in
        spring
Or the son, in the doorway, waiting for her return

LACE

blackberry bushes—
the path never made
into them

beads of water
abandoned the branches
every morning
as the sun stretched down, down for each day

—didn't it seem
just for us?

just for us
moss covered stonewall
perpendicular to the road

just for us
white daisies
plucked from the field, dyed light blue

Queen Anne's lace
from white
most delicate, and interesting
to change

CHRISTOPHER STREET

Summer, barely, I count the time shine and dirt
Of the station happen together
A young man on a wooden bench at the end of the platform
Waiting for a train, his head back sleeping

Rats among the subway tracks, sparkle and filth
I, also others, notice he's too still, too quiet
Blood lines the sides of his mouth

Looking down the worn tunnel, listening too
Waiting for the train, looking
A few more see the boy (man) not moving, bleeding
His head in an uncomfortable position

The train arrives, finally, 20 or 30 people
Into the air conditioned cars (which smell of waste)
A number look back to see
Him not move as we move

CONCERN

You had said: "I would be scared"
Quite openly admitting this over the phone

During August heat
Ice cubes melting my feet
In the bright metal mixing bowl
Soaking my toes in cool cool water

Your question
"Are you seeing anyone, romantically?"
Sifting its way

 "No, not really"
Your concern

Your genuine concern:
"I would be scared to sleep alone"

AT A LAKE

Ragged, breathless
I went to water
Cleaned the drying perch—
Bloody, headless things they turned into.

       this was years ago and I was not
       someone I know

Dull tearing sound
Knife shredding skin.

       might well have been
       every slice calling me harmful

On a white cutting board
Soaked strong sun
Innards, small harmless innards
Of what I found below a surface.

       I will not return or ever breathe
       as at a landscape

This a landscape, backdrop
Fallen, harmless, wide.

APEX

Wednesday evening, raining hard: thunderstorm right overhead, felt like climbing naked onto the fire escape and letting each drop hit me pretending hurt or bruise at least: but I lay on the bed with no clothes, instead of you: and watched the man in the apartment behind our building make himself at home: yet I did not see, except his cat frightened near the windowsill: each storm portion passed its very way by-and-by, but then I did: he had longish black curly hair, water does drip drop and hit soft: stretch and fall of humidity changes from or accumulates to: like the slow build up of a leaf jam in a culvert, it does not in the end matter how it started: just what the trouble amounted to: I am annoyed there is always process before product shouldn't it be the other way around: not necessarily opposite, just why does sudden almost never mean sudden: it happened like this or that: the slow stroke of a boomerang wasn't what I saw

AFTER DINNER

there's the dictionary
        with *-nighthawk-*
                -banshee-

-portmanteau- a word adored in its three distinct syllables
             smoke and fog equals *-smog-*

you can flip through the pages
        discover just about anything at all
                -nimbostratus Corpus Christi-

but you know,
        my mother still died alone at night

SEPTEMBER

Each tree I see
Should hold me
That's what I say

With deep leaves
Hidden branches

From the window
A chance to touch
What's touched

This wind I'm in
Keeps rushing in

BLACKOUT/SEACOAST

Dear, the flashlight's fading
This mess on the table wasn't me
Only a leak in the cheap coffee cup…

What have you thought up, this time
Our evening house arrest
Sea is leaving, earth's ballast
An infidelity, wreck and play
Turning a way, ticking to a time

Certain lovers watch the clock
You think of me what I am not
      I don't persuade otherwise
Here's the mattress, then the mistress
Sewn together two tiny letters

UNTITLED

I was touching your skin
hoping my body
could be your whole day

IMAGINE

This week my horoscope says:
"...you can still swim to safety
But you had better get moving—
The tide won't be in your favor indefinitely."
Like there's not enough pressure
I need that over my head
That's what my horoscope said

I can't take it all too seriously
In an imaginary world I wake
Flour on the bed in billows
Ready for baking
I might wander, in an elevated position
To the kitchen
Which is rooms and rooms away
From where I wake, is it not

Is it not like this, in an imaginary world
Where every step is on a surface that is comfortable
Or kind, engaging, generous
Like time is generous when we are young
Then becomes stingy

What did I do to make the world so stingy?
And how is every day just one thing
Rather than a number of things
And is this so wrong?

My horoscope also says:
"The worst possible thing you can do this week is to dither"
Dither, a harsh word
Sticks on the tongue doing what is opposite to mean

Opposite of love is hate, opposite of give is take
When one half exists without the other
I think the sky begins to shudder

for Peter Covino

CONNECTICUT

Road kill slash paper bag
Aesthetic widow's walk, excuse me
What is the purple flower, so prolific?

Under promise, name a particular mountain range
Discover covered bridges, a horse's convenience.

Church spear or town hall cupola
Create the same strain
Peddle then yearn, appear a perfect day.

AFTER LANDSCAPE

If I were to lay myself down
On a moving river
I would become as a moving river

If I were to lay myself down
On a frozen moving river
I would become cold

Let's start again
If I were to lay myself down
On a river
Moving or frozen
I would become grateful
One, moving with the river
Or two, the river moving underneath this ice
I could sense direction either way

If I were to lay myself down
On a river I could remember
What a moon or a sun looks like from a flat position
How wrapping around the landscape (earth's landscape after landscape)
We all must go somewhere

CASPIAN AT 10 PM

Lightning showing across the lake
Tendency toward mayhem, strike and curve

Prior in the day, our sail mast cracked
One slow bend

The very height of summer, never quite enough for the dip and shade
Of the tall green tree weeks to turning orange

On the south side of the cove
My nephew had formed an *L* with his body, an *O* with his mouth

Must have been thinking:
This is how I can look, this is how I can sound

Acknowledgments

Grateful acknowledgment to the editors of the following publications where several of the poems, some in different versions, first appeared:

Temper, The Breakup, China Lake, The Chore, Surgery, Maine, Untitled (Final Wave) and *Elizabeth* appeared in FOUR WAY READER #2, Four Way Books

Summer appeared in THE MARLBORO REVIEW

Gnaw and Echo of the Aircraft appeared in THE CORTLAND REVIEW

After Landscape and *Apex* appeared in 3RD BED

Starting In appeared in HELIOTROPE

At a Lake and *Blackout/Seacoast* appeared in CHARTER OAK REVIEW

Endless gratitude to Martha Rhodes for her inspiration and generosity; and with appreciation for past and ongoing support: Michael Ryan, Michael Burkard, Joan Aleshire, Alan Williamson, Jeffrey Levine, Fred Arroyo, Lois Hirshkowitz, Patricia Carlin, Dave Smith, and Larry Levis. Many thanks to family and friends, too numerous here to mention, whose encouragement and guidance has truly made everything possible. In particular, thank you to three friends: Sandra Hamlet, Rebecca Cooney, and Rachel Harris. And finally, forever thanks to Peter Covino – an exceptional friend and poet.